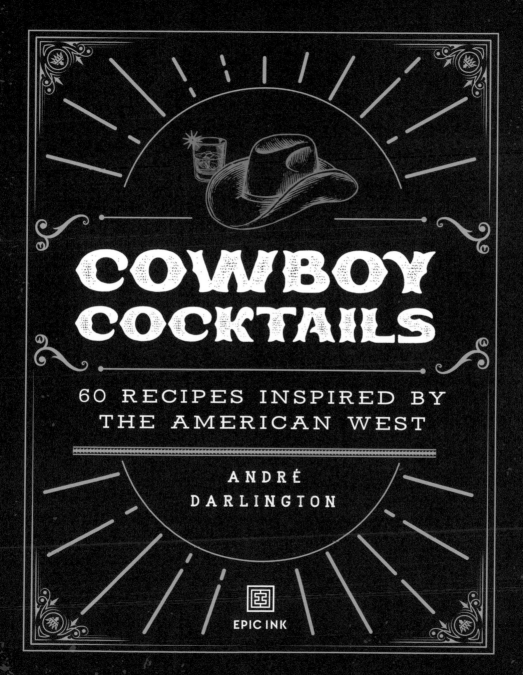

COWBOY COCKTAILS

60 RECIPES INSPIRED BY THE AMERICAN WEST

ANDRÉ DARLINGTON

EPIC INK

Library of Congress Cataloging-in-Publication
Data

Names: Darlington, André, author.
Title: Cowboy cocktails : 60 recipes inspired by the
American West / André
    Darlington.
Description: New York : Epic Ink, an imprint of
The Quarto Group 2024. |
    Includes bibliographical references and index. |
Summary: "Including
    whiskey-, bourbon-, and vodka-based cocktails,
Cowboy Cocktails features
    60 recipes inspired by American cowboy
culture"-- Provided by publisher.
Identifiers: LCCN 2023018689 (print) | LCCN
2023018690 (ebook) | ISBN
    9780760383025 (hardcover) | ISBN
9780760383032 (ebook)
Subjects: LCSH: Cocktails. | LCGFT: Cookbooks.
Classification: LCC TX951 .D369 2024 (print) |
LCC TX951 (ebook) | DDC
    641.87/4--dc23/eng/20230524
LC record available at https://lccn.loc.
gov/2023018689
LC ebook record available at https://lccn.loc.
gov/2023018690

Group Publisher: Rage Kindelsperger
Creative Director: Laura Drew
Managing Editor: Cara Donaldson
Editor: Katie McGuire
Cover and Interior Design: Amelia LeBarron
Drink and Food Styling: Cynthia Hollidge and
Noah Rosenbaum

"NEVER DRINK
UNLESS YOU'RE
ALONE OR
WITH
SOMEBODY."

~ COWBOY PROVERB

To all who hear
the Call of the West

CONTENTS

14

PART 1

COFFIN VARNISH
BUILT DRINKS

46

─ • PART 2 • ─
JOY JUICE
SHAKEN DRINKS

PART 3
RED EYE
STIRRED DRINKS

122

PART 4
ROUNDUP
COWBOY PUNCHES

······ · **PART 5** · ······

CHUCK WAGON
ENTREES AND DESSERTS

INTRODUCTION
BEND AN ELBOW

"Do what you can, with what you have, where you are."

~ THEODORE ROOSEVELT

The era that gave rise to the American cowboy was surprisingly brief, a roughly thirty-year period following the Civil War (1861–65). In those few decades, millions of surplus longhorns from Texas and environs were herded along trails cutting across the Great Plains to railheads up north, traveling by train to fast-growing cities in the East. There, the newly popular beef steak featured prominently on plates at restaurants like New York City's Delmonico's. Back on the frontier, wherever the cowboy and his hard-earned trail money went, drink followed.

At first, hardly more than tents or wagons parked at train stops with SALOON painted on their sides, bars in the cattle boomtowns came to rival the gilded drinking parlors of the big cities. "Fancy drinks," aka cocktails, had already begun to spread from west to east, following the Gold Rush in San Francisco of the 1850s. They reached Denver in the 1860s, Kansas by the 1870s, and everywhere else as the nineteenth century ended.

The story of the cowboy and mixed drinks is a tale of deprivation and excess, of lonely and sober nights working the range contrasted with wild, drunken revelry in sinful towns. Dodge City, Ogallala, Cheyenne—these are the hard-nosed spots the cattle boom built, enshrined in American lore as Sodom and Gomorrah-like outposts of gambling, prostitution, shootouts . . . and drinking.

Some might decry the recipes in this book as requiring an "educated thirst," arguing that fancy drinks are for those who put on un-cowboy-like airs. But we should recall that in the cowboy West, the poor quickly became rich—if only for a day, after receiving their wages or winning at the gambling table. A few surviving recipes tell the tale of just how far "fancy" drink of the time and place traveled; famed Deadwood Dick's preferred mix made it all the way to England and into *The Savoy Cocktail Book* (page 107). We also know from historical records that cowboys drank stone fences, champagne cocktails, Queen Charlottes, sangarees, and many other mixed drinks.

But let's be clear from the outset: the book you now hold in your dusty mitts is a bit of historical fiction. Liberties have been taken and the recipes herein are inspired by the cattle kingdom and the rough characters that existed in the final days of the frontier. Yet, every effort has been made to ensure the mixtures *could have* been enjoyed in Western saloons. The ingredients are period. Cowboy drinking dens were far better equipped far earlier than we might imagine: French brandies, Champagne, gins, bitters, fine wine, and more were readily available—if for a stiff price. It should be noted that a few cocktails in this book, such as the Stirrup Cup, Rattlesnake, Mule Skinner, and the aforementioned mix ascribed to Deadwood Dick, did exist in some fashion (which is noted in the text).

The cowboy is a powerful symbol of adventure and freedom. His days on the open range presented a life that was the exact opposite of the factory drudgery to which many Americans submitted in the late nineteenth century. This dramatization of their drink is meant to both inform and inspire, whether we are at home, sitting by a campfire, or riding across the Great Plains in search of the next adventurous watering hole.

CATTLE TALK
HOW TO USE THIS BOOK

The cocktails in this book are divided into chapters based on their method of manufacture: built in the glass, shaken, stirred, and, finally, large-format cocktails for a whole posse. In broad strokes, this taxonomy tends to order the drinks in the book from lighter to more spirituous (though there are notable exceptions). Looking for something to kick off a gathering or suitable for a backyard barbecue? These are likely found in Chapter 1—see Belly Through the Brush (page 24) or Buffalo Gap (page 19)—and Chapter 4, which features four punches for a crowd.

Because shaken drinks include citrus juice, they lean toward being more refreshing cocktails; sample a Tiger's Tail (page 75) or try Salt Lick on Doe Run (page 55). Beware that because this collection is meant for cowboys, even the shaken drinks herein can bite—for instance, the Rattlesnake (page 84). Stirred drinks by and large contain only spirits and liqueurs, so they tend to be the strongest cocktails; think Manhattans, martinis, and negronis. Sample the Jack of Diamonds (page 96) and Bone Orchard (page 111) for a Wild West take on familiar mixes.

Chapter 5 includes essential chuck wagon recipes for feeding famished buckaroos. Ranch Beans, Corn Dodgers, and Chili Con Carne make for mighty fine cocktail fare. Additionally, sample period desserts such as Spotted Pup or a wowing Eggless Cake.

FLUID OUNCES	CUPS / TABLESPOONS	METRIC
16 ounces	2 cups	480 milliliters
12 ounces	1½ cups	360 milliliters
8 ounces	1 cup	240 milliliters
6 ounces	¾ cup	180 milliliters
5 ounces	1 cup + 2 tablespoons	150 milliliters
4 ounces	½ cup	120 milliliters
3 ounces	6 tablespoons	90 milliliters
2 ounces	¼ cup	60 milliliters
1 ounce	⅛ cup/2 tablespoons	30 milliliters
¾ ounce	1½ tablespoons	22.5 milliliters
½ ounce	1 tablespoon	15 milliliters

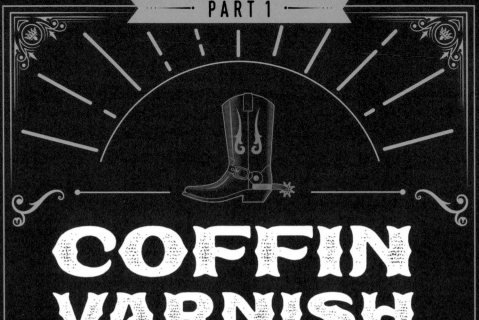

PART 1

COFFIN VARNISH

BUILT DRINKS

"THE FASCINATION OF A HORSE AND A SADDLE
WAS TOO STRONG TO BE RESISTED . . .
I TOOK TO THE RANGE
AS A PREACHER'S SON TAKES TO VICE."

ANDY ADAMS,
THE LOG OF A COWBOY

The drinks in this chapter are a combination of cocktails constructed in the glass over ice as well as those that require a bit of muddling or other handiwork. Classic built drinks include old fashioneds, sazeracs, and juleps—but also highballs and many beer cocktails. For this reason, you will find in this section both summer-y delectations, such as Watermelon Ranch Water (page 27), and gritty numbers like Dead Man's Hand (page 20). And, should you require a little warming-up on a cold night, this is where you will encounter the hot drinks Prairie Schooner (page 43) and Lucky Horseshoe (page 44).

 Stirrup Cup

Served while customers remained astride their horses, stirrup cups were an old tradition descended from drinks enjoyed before the hunt in England. The cups traveled to the New World, where they were popular at colonial taverns and, later, in the trail tents that served as early bars. Think of the service as the cowboy version of a drive-in. If the rider did dismount, he or she was given a receipt for the animal, just like modern valet parking.

Maraschino cherries appeared on US shores in 1890 and their inclusion would have marked this as a "fancy" drink. Cowboys dreamed of such treats while enduring the hardships of the open range and consumed them with relish when the opportunity arose.

INGREDIENTS

Sugar cube

2 dashes Angostura bitters

1 ounce brandy

1 ounce bourbon whiskey

Maraschino cherry, for garnish

DIRECTIONS

Add the sugar cube to a rocks glass and muddle with the bitters. Add the brandy, whiskey, and a large ice cube. Stir, then garnish with a cherry.

THE BEEF STEAK CRAZE

Millions of cattle took the railroad from Abilene, Kansas, to booming cities in the east between 1866 and 1889. During that time—roughly coinciding with the Gilded Age—the great American steak became popular, largely through the efforts of the three Delmonico restaurants in New York City. Because the establishment's famed steak was created nearly two hundred years ago (before cuts became standardized), a "Delmonico" steak today varies by region. It is frequently approximated with a New York strip.

BUFFALO GAP

Situated south of Abilene, Texas, Buffalo Gap is named for a break in the hills of the Callahan Divide. A spot where buffalo passed through for millennia, the gap also served as a convenient opening for cowboys and their cattle. Today, Buffalo Gap sports a historic village.

Note there are two cowboy-related Abilenes: Abilene, Kansas, the famous railroad trailhead where cattle were shipped east, and Abilene, Texas, which was named after the Kansas city in 1881. This refreshing take on the once-popular mix of beer and ginger beer will slack thirst no matter which dusty Abilene you are driving at. In range bars, whiskey was fifty cents and beer was twenty-five cents.

INGREDIENTS

Chile-lime salt and lime wedge, for the glass rim (such as Tajin, or use recipe to the right)
6 ounces lager-style beer
6 ounces ginger beer
Lime wedge, for garnish

DIRECTIONS

Rim a pint glass with the chile-lime salt. Add the beer and ginger beer to the glass and garnish with the fresh lime wedge.

FOR THE CHILE-LIME SALT

INGREDIENTS

¼ cup (71 g) flaky sea salt, such as Maldon
2 tablespoons freshly grated lime zest
2 teaspoons chile powder

DIRECTIONS

In a small bowl, combine the salt, lime zest, and chile powder and use immediately.

Dead Man's Hand

Famed lawman and gambler Wild Bill Hickok violated his own safety rule and sat with his back to the door in a Deadwood saloon on August 2, 1876. It was a fatal mistake, and he was shot in the back of the head by Jack McCall while holding two black aces and two black eights—posthumously known as the "dead man's hand." Bill liked whiskey for its medicinal properties and would have enjoyed this smoky and spicy Old Fashioned variation. Notable as one of the most infamous gunslingers of the West, Hickok was also inducted into the Poker Hall of Fame in 1979 for his final hand.

INGREDIENTS

2 ½ ounces bourbon whiskey

¼ ounce agave nectar

1 dash spicy bitters (such as Hella Smoked Chili bitters)

1 dash Peychaud's bitters

DIRECTIONS

In a rocks glass, combine the whiskey, agave nectar, and bitters. Add a large ice cube, give it a quick stir, and serve.

Frontier Scamper Juice

Full-fledged saloons developed from the tent bars that followed the construction of the railroad. These early establishments served whatever liquor they had on hand and weren't afraid to adulterate it to make it stretch. A common mix featured a rank combination of whiskey, molasses, tobacco, and red peppers that was variably dubbed Tarantula Juice, Neck Oil, Taos Dynamite, Popskull, Widow-Maker, and Frontier Scamper Juice. This cocktail recreates the original rotgut mix in a mighty palatable—and even downright tasty—form.

INGREDIENTS

2 ounces overproof rye whiskey
  (such as Old Overholt)

1 ounce apple cider

1 barspoon molasses

1 dash Angostura bitters

1 dash tobacco bitters (such as
  18.21 Bitters)

Lemon twist, for garnish

DIRECTIONS

In a rocks glass, combine the whiskey, cider, molasses, and bitters. Stir until the molasses is dissolved, add a large ice cube, and garnish with a lemon twist.

Belly Through the Brush

A saying that meant "to dodge the law," bellying through the brush was a common enough practice for a cowboy after they got into trouble while on a break from the trail. Cow towns boasted all sorts of diversions, and trouble followed all the drinking and gambling. There's plenty of brush to belly through in this cocktail, which features the underappreciated combination of tequila and mint.

INGREDIENTS

8 mint leaves

½ lime, cut into wedges

½ ounce agave nectar

2 ounces reposado tequila

2 ounces club soda

DIRECTIONS

Muddle the mint, lime wedges, and agave nectar in a rocks glass. Add a large ice cube, the tequila, and the soda, and stir.

WATERMELON RANCH WATER

"Ranch water" is the name for the combination of tequila, lime juice, and sparkling water. Add watermelon agua fresca into the mix and you have an improved version that positively sings in the desert heat. This drink is an excellent accompaniment to cowboy grub of all kinds. Watermelon is one of the easiest fruits to employ in cocktails and can be added by muddling and straining (or not), or by using the juice-making method below.

INGREDIENTS

2 ounces blanco tequila

½ ounce fresh lime juice

3 ounces fresh watermelon juice
(see recipe to the right)

2 ounces Topo Chico (or club soda)

Watermelon wedge, for garnish

DIRECTIONS

Combine the tequila, lime juice, watermelon juice, and Topo Chico in a highball or other tall glass and stir. Garnish with a watermelon wedge.

FOR THE WATERMELON JUICE

Place some slices (rinds removed) or chunks of watermelon in a blender and blend. If the result is too pulpy, strain through a sieve. Alternatively, chunks of watermelon can be juiced in the glass with a muddler.

G·T·T· G&T

G.T.T. stands for "gone to Texas." During the financial panic of 1819, Americans from Southern states emigrated to Texas in order to flee bankruptcy and debt. At the time, Texas was part of Mexico and thus provided a safe haven and a fresh start. How did you know if your neighbor had abandoned their farmstead for happier climes? They'd chalk "G.T.T." above the doorway or on a fencepost. Eventually, G.T.T. became associated with anyone on the outs with the law.

Gin in the early range days was not today's London Dry style, but rather Old Tom or even gin's precursor, Genever. Both Old Tom and Genever are widely available in liquor stores today and are worth exploring. Beware: this recipe kicks like a mule team on its way to Texas—in a good way.

INGREDIENTS

2 ½ ounces Old Tom gin
(or Genever)

5 ounces tonic water

4 black peppercorns

10 red pepper flakes

Lemon twist, for garnish

DIRECTIONS

In a wine or rocks glass, combine some ice with the gin, tonic water, peppercorns, and red pepper flakes. Garnish with a lemon twist.

THAT OLD TOM GIN

Gin was popular in the US during the post-
Civil War cowboy era, but the prevailing
style in the mid- to late nineteenth
century was Old Tom, a sweeter, softer
version than the style we know today.
Old Tom gins appeared in cocktail books
(and saloons) of the time, but they were
eventually supplanted by London Dry gins
such as Tanqueray and Beefeater. Luckily,
Old Tom gins have seen a resurgence in
recent years. Hayman's Old Tom gin is a
fine example and is widely available in
liquor stores and online.

Trail Cutter

A trail cutter is a cowboy who searches for strays among a moving herd of cattle. In modern times, the practice is a competition sport, but it had real application on the range whenever two herds co-mingled in a stampede.

Shrubs—the drink, not the plants—are an old way to preserve fruits out of season. The term comes from the Arabic word *sharab*, meaning "to drink." The trick is to muddle fruit in a mix of sugar and vinegar, resulting in a complex taste that is fantastic in cocktails. Cowboys foraged for all sorts of berries along the trail, such as currants, wild strawberries, muscadines, and blackberries. Fruit was eaten in season, dried, or, if lucky, consumed in a shrub with liquor.

INGREDIENTS

2 ounces bourbon whiskey

1 ounce Blueberry Shrub (see recipe to the right)

4 ounces club soda

Rosemary sprig, for garnish

DIRECTIONS

In a highball glass filled with ice, combine the whiskey, Blueberry Shrub, and club soda. Stir and garnish with a sprig of rosemary.

FOR THE BLUEBERRY SHRUB

INGREDIENTS

2 cups (220 g) blueberries

1 cup (200 g) granulated sugar

1 cup (230 g) apple cider vinegar

DIRECTIONS

In a medium bowl, muddle the blueberries. Add the sugar and stir together until combined. Cover and let macerate overnight at room temperature. Using a cheesecloth or strainer, squeeze the juice from the blueberries into a sealable jar and add the vinegar. Stir, then store, refrigerated, for up to two weeks.

GOODNIGHT LOVING

No, this cocktail is not named for a moment of late-night passion; Charles Goodnight and Oliver Loving (made famous in the book-turned-film *Lonesome Dove*) were the first to drive their longhorn cattle from Texas all the way to Wyoming. This was the start of the famed Goodnight-Loving Trail. Apple cider was a popular and readily available ingredient and Stone Fences (apple cider mixed with whiskey or rum) were a well-known offering in frontier saloons. This is a fancier version, fit for a cowboy who just made his earnings.

INGREDIENTS

1 ½ ounces brandy

4 ounces apple cider

¼ ounce fresh lemon juice

1 dash Peychaud's bitters, for garnish

Lemon slice, for garnish

DIRECTIONS

In a highball glass filled with ice, combine the brandy, apple cider, and lemon juice. Garnish with bitters and a lemon slice.

White Mule

White whiskey, also called white mule or moonshine, commonly refers to whiskey straight from the still that has not seen a barrel. Davy Crockett called it "green whiskey" and legend has it he drank a horn of the stuff in one swallow at a Little Rock bar on the way to the Alamo. He claimed it was so hot he no longer needed to have his food cooked—it got burned on the way to his stomach. Moonshine, or white whiskey, is now widely available in liquor stores. More than a novelty, it imparts a unique flavor to cocktails.

INGREDIENTS

2 ounces white whiskey

½ ounce fresh lime juice

3 ounces ginger beer

1 dash Angostura bitters

DIRECTIONS

In a rocks glass or copper mug filled with ice, combine the whiskey, lime juice, ginger beer, and Angostura bitters.

Cast-Iron Julep

A slice of peach stewed in whiskey was once a fairly frequent addition in juleps. In fact, homemade peach brandy was likely used in a pinch when other liquor was not available. The tradition is honored in this recipe with a grilled peach slice, which lends nice smoky and caramelized notes to the classic drink. Pro tip: Grill peaches when the fruits are in season and freeze them for later use all year long. This drink is ideal around a campfire but works for any occasion.

INGREDIENTS

6 mint leaves

½ ounce simple syrup

2 grilled peach slices (see recipe to the right)

2 ½ ounces bourbon whiskey

Mint sprig, for garnish

DIRECTIONS

In a julep cup or rocks glass, muddle the mint and simple syrup. Add the grilled peach slices, whiskey, and crushed ice, and garnish with a mint sprig. Serve with a cobbler spoon (a metal straw with a small round spoon attached, sometimes called a spoon straw).

FOR THE GRILLED PEACHES

INGREDIENTS

6 peaches

1 ounce olive oil

DIRECTIONS

Prepare the grill for direct grilling. Halve the peaches and remove the pits. Brush the cut side with olive oil and grill cut-side down, over medium heat, for 4 to 5 minutes. Flip the peaches and cook for 4 to 5 minutes more, or until they have softened and the skin has charred.

 Madame Mustache

At one time, saloons offered complimentary towels hanging at intervals along the front of the bar, so cowboys could wipe beer suds from their mustaches. But this cocktail is named for one Eleanor Dumont, known later in life as Madame Mustache. A petite and charming French woman, renowned for being quick with a horsewhip and a pistol, she operated a series of gambling dens across the western frontier. Having lost her looks after a long and colorful career (and gaining her moniker due to healthy growth on her top lip), Madame Dumont ended her days with a cocktail—of Champagne and prussic acid. Salute the famed female fair dealer with this frothy mix that lifts beer to the sublime.

* · ✳ · *

INGREDIENTS

1 ½ ounces mezcal

¾ ounce agave nectar

3 dashes Angostura bitters

12 ounces lager-style beer

DIRECTIONS

In a chilled pint or highball glass, combine the mezcal, agave nectar, Angostura bitters, and beer.

Necktie Social

Cattle rustlers posed a big problem on the frontier and were summarily dealt with by hanging from the closest cottonwood tree. Often a posse was assembled for the work, and, due to their gallows humor, cowboys dubbed the affairs "necktie socials." Based on a period punch, this is a decadent and esteemed assemblage of liquor that would fit such a festive occasion.

INGREDIENTS

1 ounce aged rum

1 ounce bourbon whiskey

½ ounce brandy

½ ounce simple syrup

Lemon slice, for garnish

Mint sprig, for garnish

DIRECTIONS

In a wine glass or julep cup filled with crushed ice, combine the rum, whiskey, and brandy. Stir, add more ice, top with simple syrup, and garnish with a lemon slice and sprig of mint. Serve with a straw or cobbler spoon.

FAMOUS FRONTIER LAWMEN

Sheriff Pat Garrett killed Billy the Kid. Bass Reeves served as a US marshal for thirty-two years and captured three thousand outlaws during his illustrious career. Bill Tilghman, Chris Madsen, and Heck Thomas became known as the Three Guardsmen because of their collective success in bringing criminals to justice. The famed Bat Masterson survived his stint as a lawman in Dodge City and became a sports writer in New York City. Even Wild Bill Hickok took a shift with the star on his chest. However, by far the most famous frontier lawman was Wyatt Earp, who took part in the most famous gunfight in the Old West, the shootout at the O.K. Corral (see page 120).

Prairie Schooner

It is estimated that nearly half a million Americans traveled west by wagon in the mid-nineteenth century. Constructed with six or seven curved wooden bows supporting a canvas cover, the wagons resembled a sailing ship. These wagons carried all a family's possessions and provided a place to sleep on the open range. The wagons were also used as commissaries to feed traveling workers such as cowboys (see page 133). While granulated sugar was a rare treat, honey could sometimes be found along the trail. This warm cocktail is ideal after a long rainy day on horseback.

INGREDIENTS

2 ounces bourbon whiskey

1 ounce honey

4 ounces hot water

Lemon wedge, for garnish

DIRECTIONS

In a mug, combine the whiskey, honey, and hot water. Stir, then garnish with a lemon wedge.

Lucky Horseshoe

There was no shortage of both Irish cowboys and outlaws in the West (Billy the Kid was born Henry McCarty). In fact, Montana at one time was envisioned as a kind of "New Ireland" by General Thomas Meagher. Jameson whiskey arrived with the many immigrants from the Green Isle as early as 1780. What became known as Irish coffee likely originated in the 1940s, but we can imagine that plenty of drovers added whiskey to coffee much earlier. Let's play make-believe and bring some period ingredients together (Southern Comfort was born in 1874 in New Orleans). Consume this magic mix and you will find yourself lucky indeed.

INGREDIENTS

1 ½ ounces Irish whiskey

¼ ounce molasses

6 ounces hot coffee

Southern Comfort whipped cream
(see recipe to the right)

DIRECTIONS

In a warm mug, stir together the whiskey, molasses, and coffee. Top with the Southern Comfort whipped cream.

FOR THE SOUTHERN COMFORT WHIPPED CREAM

INGREDIENTS

2 cups (470 g) whipping cream

2 tablespoons powdered sugar

3 tablespoons Southern Comfort

DIRECTIONS

Place a whipped cream dispenser (iSi's is recommended) in the refrigerator for at least 2 hours or until chilled. Add all the ingredients to the dispenser and mix thoroughly, then screw on the lid and shake 3 to 5 times. Alternatively,

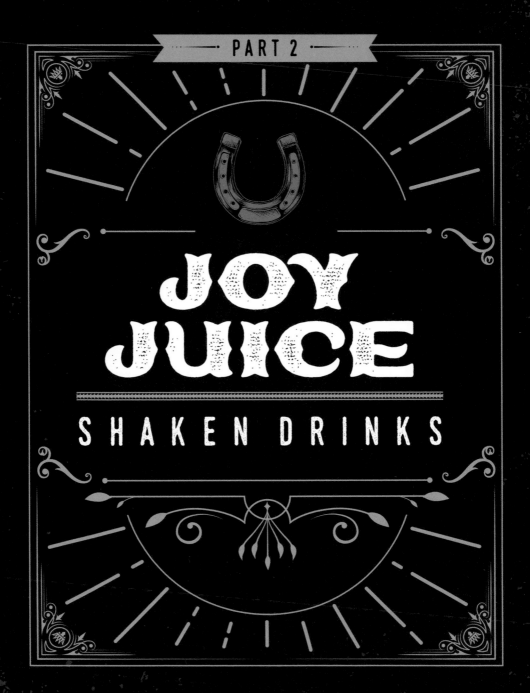

PART 2

JOY JUICE

SHAKEN DRINKS

"SAID ARISTOTLE UNTO PLATO, 'HAVE ANOTHER SWEET POTATO?' SAID PLATO UNTO ARISTOTLE, 'THANK YOU, I PREFER THE BOTTLE.'"

OWEN WISTER, AUTHOR OF *THE VIRGINIAN*

Cocktails are typically shaken when they contain citrus, eggs, or dairy (for egg substitutes, see page 159). Shaking aerates and emulsifies the drink in addition to chilling it. Famous drinks that are shaken include daiquiris, Bloody Marys, and margaritas, as well as egg and cream drinks such as flips. Because shaken drinks contain non-alcoholic elements such as citrus juice, they tend to be more refreshing and lower in ABV (alcohol by volume) than their spirituous, stirred cousins. In this section you will find cowboy takes on the popular whiskey sour and margarita variations, but also many genuinely new cowboy concoctions. Because they were not brought along on the trail, eggs were highly prized and sought after whenever there was a chance to consume them; the egg cocktails in this section make up for lost time with a few genuine cactus bangers that use them to thrilling effect.

SWING RIDER

A swing rider stuck close to the side of a herd, about one-third of the way back from the point rider at the front. They took a key position, ensuring that a herd could turn properly while also filling in for the point rider when necessary. After a successful day on the lookout for cattle trying to break away, enjoy this rewarding combination of whiskey and ginger. This is a reliable and satisfying cocktail for a skillful cowboy. Canton ginger liqueur is widely available in liquor stores and is a trusty addition to any home bar.

INGREDIENTS

1 ½ ounces bourbon whiskey

1 ounce Canton ginger liqueur

½ ounce fresh lemon juice

Lemon twist, for garnish

DIRECTIONS

Shake the whiskey, ginger liqueur, and lemon juice with ice. Strain into a cocktail glass and garnish with a lemon twist.

TONTO RIM

Tonto means "dumb" or "foolish" in Spanish, and Arizona's Tonto Rim is named after a Native American group dubbed the Tonto Apaches. Why they were so-named has been lost to history, but theories suggest either the group spoke a different Apache dialect or, more simply, that messing with these particular Apaches was stupid. The Rim is featured in a number of cowboy stories, including the Zane Grey novel *Under the Tonto Rim*, which was made into a film in 1947. Create your own rim with this salt-lined refresher that works equally well with a barbecue or at brunch.

INGREDIENTS

Sea salt, for the glass rim

2 ounces blanco tequila

5 ounces fresh grapefruit juice

¼ ounce fresh lime juice

Lime wedge, for garnish

DIRECTIONS

Rim a highball glass with salt. Shake the tequila, grapefruit juice, and lime juice with ice. Strain into the prepared glass filled with ice and garnish with a lime wedge.

 Broncobuster

Breaking a wild horse to the saddle was no easy feat, and if someone was good at it, their acclaim spread quickly. A cowboy fighting to stay aboard a bucking bronco is one of the most famous images of the West, cast into the American imagination by the sculptor Frederic Remington. Fun fact: Remington used a sketch by Theodore Roosevelt (drawn before he was president) as inspiration. Think of this cocktail as a sports drink designed for those arduous first rides.

INGREDIENTS

1 ounce Old Tom gin

¾ ounce dry curaçao

¾ ounce French vermouth

¾ ounce fresh lemon juice

¼ ounce agave syrup

Lemon peel, for garnish

DIRECTIONS

Shake the gin, curaçao, vermouth, lemon juice, and agave syrup with ice. Strain into a cocktail glass and garnish with a lemon peel.

THE COWBOY PRESIDENT

Teddy Roosevelt's mother and wife died only hours apart in 1884. The loss left the young future president inconsolable, and he left his home and work for the Dakota Territories a few months later. Roosevelt's time in the West as a rancher (and, briefly, as a sheriff) influenced the remainder of his life. He led cavalry in the Spanish–American War in a regiment dubbed the "Rough Riders," a name lifted from Buffalo Bill's traveling Western show. Roosevelt's deep ties to the frontier also led him to become one of America's greatest conservationists.

Salt Lick on Doe Run

Deer (and humans) need salt for growth and survival. In fact, humans need 500 mg of salt a day to keep the nervous system and muscles functioning normally. Natural salt licks play an important role in providing animals with much-needed minerals such as zinc, iron, phosphorus, and calcium. Cattle need salt, too, and known deer licks were a good resource for cowboys and their herds. Give this hibiscus margarita a lick and replenish.

INGREDIENTS

Sea salt, for the glass rim

1 ½ ounces reposado tequila

1 ounce fresh lime juice

1 ounce Hibiscus Syrup (see recipe to the right)

1 dash Peychaud's bitters

DIRECTIONS

Salt the rim of a rocks or highball glass. Shake the tequila, lime juice, Hibiscus Syrup, and bitters with ice and pour into the prepared glass.

FOR THE HIBISCUS SYRUP

INGREDIENTS

1 cup (237 g) water

1 cup (200 g) sugar

½ cup (13 g) dried hibiscus petals

DIRECTIONS

In a small saucepan, bring the water to a boil. Remove from heat, add the sugar, and stir to combine. Add the hibiscus and let steep for 15 minutes. Strain into a sealable jar. Hibiscus Syrup will keep up to two weeks, sealed, in the refrigerator.

Big Fifty

The Sharps "Big Fifty" rifle was one of the iconic guns of the Old West. It featured an incredible range for both keeping enemies at bay and hunting buffalo. It weighed sixteen pounds unloaded and was durable, practical, and accurate. This heady concoction offers a similar big bang. Champagne was readily available in mining and cattle towns for celebrating finds, gambling wins, or the end of a drive. Bubbly was also brought on trains to slake the thirst of many an East Coast millionaire exploring the West from the comfort of their sleeping car.

INGREDIENTS

1 ounce bourbon whiskey

½ ounce dry curaçao

½ ounce fresh lemon juice

1 barspoon simple syrup

3 ounces sparkling wine

Orange peel, for garnish

DIRECTIONS

Shake the whiskey, curaçao, lemon juice, and simple syrup with ice. Strain into a cocktail glass and top with sparkling wine. Garnish with an orange peel.

Green Cloth

Gamblers were flashy dressers and usually good with a knife and a pistol—their well-being depended on it. Life upon the green cloth was mercurial and often brief. Gambling was an obsession in cowboy country, and serving alcohol at a bar was secondary to the primary business: separating rubes from their hard-earned dinero. To ensure good luck, gamblers resorted to various talismans to ensure fortune's favor, a popular one being the heart of a bat tied to the right sleeve. Kick back from the table with this luxurious green cocktail.

INGREDIENTS

2 ounces reposado tequila

1 ounce fresh lime juice

½ ounce simple syrup

¼ ounce chartreuse

1 dash orange bitters

Lime peel, for garnish

DIRECTIONS

Shake the tequila, lime juice, simple syrup, chartreuse, and bitters with ice and strain into a cocktail glass. Garnish with a lime peel.

POWDER RIVER WAR

The Powder River War, also called the Johnson County War (see sidebar), was a range war from 1889 to 1893 that marked the end of the cowboy era. Rue the ignominious end of the hardworking cowboy with this orgeat cocktail. Orgeat, a complex almond-inflected syrup, was sometimes employed as a substitute in the Old West for fresh citrus, which was often unavailable.

INGREDIENTS

1 ounce blended Scotch
1 ounce rye whiskey
½ ounce Grand Marnier
¾ ounce Orgeat (see recipe to the right)
¼ ounce fresh lemon juice

DIRECTIONS

Shake the Scotch, whiskey, Grand Marnier, Orgeat, and lemon juice with ice. Strain into a cocktail glass.

FOR THE ORGEAT

Makes approximately 1 cup (245 g)

INGREDIENTS

½ cup (100 g) granulated sugar
Peel of half a grapefruit
1 scant cup (245 g) almond milk (preferably Silk Original)
8 drops almond extract
4 drops orange flower water

DIRECTIONS

In a medium-sized sealable jar, macerate the sugar and grapefruit peel for 1 to 2 hours. Add the almond milk and remove the peel. Add the almond extract and orange flower water and shake the mixture until the sugar dissolves. Orgeat will keep, sealed, in the refrigerator for about a week.

JOHNSON COUNTY WAR

The so-called Johnson County War began when large cattle companies started to target supposed rustlers in Wyoming, including hanging innocent Ella Watson and her husband without trial. The incident culminated in a number of the state's wealthiest and most prominent citizens hiring gunmen to assassinate Sheriff Red Angus and his deputy, the county commissioners, and any other locals who opposed them (and who were attempting to uphold the law). The war ultimately pitted the Cattle Barons against the cowboys who worked for them and led to an intervention by President Harrison.

 # VELVET COUCH

A cowboy's bedroll was his one earthly possession and it journeyed along the trail with him in the accompanying chuck wagon. Civil War-era, army-issued bedrolls could weigh sixty pounds or more, and were filled with rain gear, food, dirty laundry, and extra spurs. The joke, of course, is that lying on the dusty roll on the rocky ground was "no velvet couch." This drink is both plush and white as new snow. Gin on the range after the Civil War would likely have been Genever or Old Tom, but any style will work in this cocktail.

INGREDIENTS

2 ounces Genever

½ ounce dry curaçao

½ ounce fresh lemon juice

¼ ounce simple syrup

1 egg white

3 dashes orange bitters,
   for garnish

DIRECTIONS

Shake the Genever, curaçao, lemon juice, simple syrup, and egg white vigorously with ice. Strain into a cocktail glass and garnish with orange bitters.

Thorny Rose

Thorny Rose was the bandit queen of the West. Born Laura Bullion, the able thief and cross-dresser was a famed member of Butch Cassidy's Wild Bunch. After raiding a bank in New Mexico in 1899, the gang hid out in a brothel in San Antonio. The cash crop of the famed San Antonio Missions (see sidebar) at one time was cochineal, the cactus-eating insect used to dye clothes, paints, and liqueurs such as Campari. Enjoy this crimson historical mashup in honor of a true femme fatale. Note that while Campari no longer employs cochineal to color its product, Bruto Americano by St. George Spirits still does, and is superb in this drink.

INGREDIENTS

1 ½ ounces reposado tequila

2 ounces fresh grapefruit juice

1 ounce Campari or Bruto
   Americano

1 barspoon rose water

Rose petal, for garnish (optional)

DIRECTIONS

Shake the tequila, grapefruit juice, Campari or Bruto Americano, and rose water with ice. Strain into a cocktail glass and garnish with a rose petal, if you like.

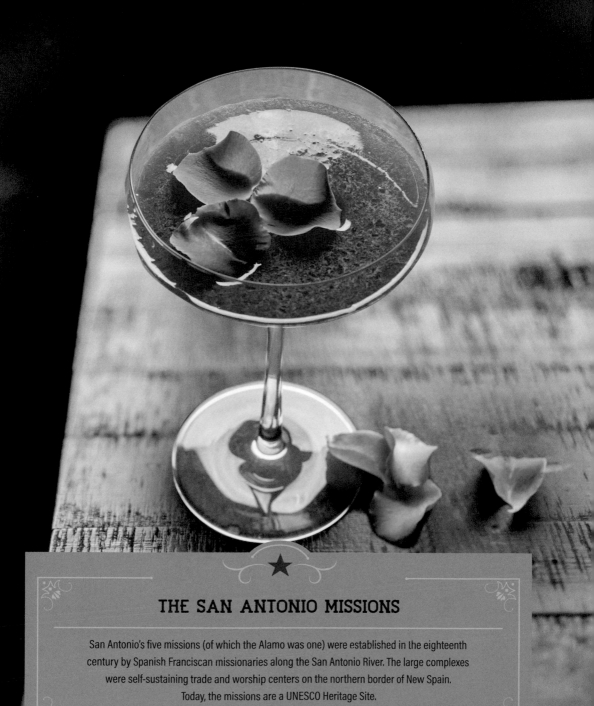

THE SAN ANTONIO MISSIONS

San Antonio's five missions (of which the Alamo was one) were established in the eighteenth
century by Spanish Franciscan missionaries along the San Antonio River. The large complexes
were self-sustaining trade and worship centers on the northern border of New Spain.
Today, the missions are a UNESCO Heritage Site.

CIMARRON

The Cimarron River flows through four states, from New Mexico to Kansas. It was known as the Red River to cowboys because its red-clay banks colored the water. The Chisholm Trail crossed the Cimarron south of Dodge City, and the river was a dangerous obstacle when it was swollen. While gunfights get the press and popular attention, river crossings posed the gravest threat to cowboys.

Using fruit preserves in mixed drinks is an old bartender's trick and any jam in your pantry is fair game. Strawberries are a great choice with agave spirits, providing an especially winning foil for smoky mezcal.

INGREDIENTS

2 ounces reposado tequila
½ ounce mezcal
½ ounce fresh lime juice

1 heaping barspoon
   strawberry preserves
Strawberry, for garnish
   (optional)

DIRECTIONS

Shake the tequila, mezcal, lime juice, and strawberry preserves with ice. Strain into a cocktail glass and garnish with a strawberry, if you like.

Boss
of the Plains

Legend has it John Stetson was in Colorado looking for gold when he made himself an all-weather hat by boiling animal fur, a rudimentary form of felting that did not require tanning the hide. By 1865, he was mass-producing the prototype and the Stetson went on to become the best-selling hat of all time. The style proved so popular that by 1902 a nine-acre facility in Philadelphia was producing the iconic cowboy attire. This soft cocktail with golden orgeat (Stetson emblazoned his name in gold stitching inside each hat) is just the right mix for donning a standard four-inch crown and four-inch rim "ten-gallon"—likely named after a corruption of the Spanish *tan galán*, which meant "very handsome."

INGREDIENTS

2 ounces reposado tequila

½ ounce fresh lime juice

½ ounce Orgeat (page 60)

½ ounce heavy cream

DIRECTIONS

Shake the tequila, lime juice, Orgeat and cream with ice. Strain into a cocktail glass.

Ol' Snakehead

Cheap and strong, frontier liquor was highly adulterated. Anything and everything was added that would help a bartender make a claim as to its potency. What's stronger than a rattlesnake head? In fact, there may have been enough rattlesnake heads floating in whiskey jars in the West to make the connection explicit; cowboy accounts of the time also call whiskey "snakehead," the two names being practically interchangeable. This is a more refreshing take on the original, the serpent being replaced by cucumber. It's a novel pairing that works.

INGREDIENTS

2 cucumber slices, plus 1
    for garnish
2 ounces bourbon whiskey

¾ ounce fresh lemon juice
½ ounce simple syrup

DIRECTIONS

Muddle cucumber slices and shake with whiskey, lemon juice, simple syrup, and ice. Strain into a rocks glass with a large ice cube and garnish with a cucumber slice.

BUCKAROO

The term "buckaroo" comes from a corruption of the Spanish word for cowboy, *vaquero*. It first appeared in American English in 1827. And it wasn't just the word that American cowboys borrowed from the Spanish, but also the style of lassoing cattle with a rope. Lasso comes from the Spanish word *lazo*, meaning noose. Oranges were thought to have medicinal value, and likely the only times a cowboy would see one was if he were sick.

INGREDIENTS

2 ounces blanco tequila

1 ½ ounces fresh orange juice

½ ounce fresh lemon juice

¼ ounce Luxardo maraschino liqueur

Maraschino cherry, for garnish (optional)

DIRECTIONS

Shake the tequila, orange juice, lemon juice, and maraschino liqueur with ice and strain into a cocktail glass. Garnish with a cherry, if you like.

 # TIGER'S TAIL

Faro was one of the most popular card games in the West. The deck was played by the dealer out of a box with the image of a tiger on it. This explains why "twisting the tiger's tail" became a euphemism for gambling. Fancy drinks were the order of the day in gambling saloons, and gin would have been available at a premium for winners getting smiled upon by Lady Luck.

INGREDIENTS

1 ½ ounces gin
½ ounce dry curaçao
½ ounce fresh lime juice

¼ ounce Hibiscus Syrup
(page 55)
Orange peel, for garnish

DIRECTIONS

Shake the gin, curaçao, lime juice, and Hibiscus Syrup with ice. Strain into a cocktail glass and garnish with an orange peel.

SLEEPING WEASEL

To "catch a weasel asleep" was a cowboy saying that referred to something unlikely or impossible. It was used in regard to especially alert cowboys (or gunslingers) who one simply couldn't catch off guard, i.e.: "You couldn't fool that guy at cards any sooner than you'd catch a weasel asleep." Eggs were a luxury that seldom featured in a cowboy meal. They were a chief motivation—along with alcohol, music, and gambling—to ride into town.

INGREDIENTS

1 ounce gin

1 ounce watermelon juice

½ ounce fresh lemon juice

½ ounce simple syrup

1 egg white

2 dashes Peychaud's bitters,
   for garnish

DIRECTIONS

Shake the gin, watermelon juice, lemon juice, simple syrup, and egg white vigorously with ice. Strain into a cocktail glass and garnish with bitters.

BARBED WIRE

Farmer Joseph Glidden of DeKalb, Illinois, filed a patent for barbed wire in 1873. Sales of the new fencing took off when an enterprising young man named John Warne Gates created a corral in the center of San Antonio. By 1880, some 80 million pounds of barbed wire were being produced and its widespread adoption meant the end of cattle trails, cowboys, and the open range.

Devil's Rope

The invention of barbed wire, or devil's rope as it was called, signaled the end of the frontier. When small homesteaders started portioning off the range, it became increasingly difficult to drive cattle through to market. Some big ranches adapted and adopted barbed-wire fences themselves, but this meant the demise of the cowboy.

Thorny blackberries were introduced into the US in the nineteenth century and spread aggressively. The tasty fruits are used to make crème de mûre (think Kir Royales), a liqueur that is delightful in cocktails. Here it summons up the devil's rope crisscrossing the frontier—and becomes the perfect match for tequila.

INGREDIENTS

2 ounces reposado tequila

¾ ounce fresh lemon juice

1 ounce crème de mûre

1 dash Angostura bitters

1 dash Peychaud's bitters

Lemon slice, for garnish

DIRECTIONS

Shake the tequila, lemon juice, crème de mûre, and bitters with ice. Strain into a cocktail or small rocks glass and garnish with a lemon slice.

Grand Hazard

Grand Hazard was one of the most popular frontier games. It was played with two dice, like modern craps, and is so old it is mentioned in Chaucer's *Canterbury Tales*. Dice games followed wherever there was money to be made and lost, and Grand Hazard was popular in the boomtowns of Deadwood, Virginia City, Dodge City, and Tombstone. Port made an early appearance in the West because it transports easily and keeps well. Here it is employed as a float on top of a whiskey sour.

INGREDIENTS

1 ½ ounces rye whiskey

¾ ounce fresh lemon juice

½ ounce simple syrup

1 ounce tawny port

DIRECTIONS

Shake the whiskey, lemon juice, and simple syrup with ice. Strain into a rocks glass with a large ice cube and, using the back of a barspoon, float the port on top.

The Alamo City

The first big cattle drives on the Chisholm Trail north originated south of San Antonio and passed through in 1866, a year after the end of the Civil War. As the fountainhead of the trail, the Alamo City played a central role in the cowboy era. Today, a Heritage Parade and drive still marks the beginning of rodeo season. Think of this cocktail as the earliest version of a root beer float—all frothy deliciousness. Sarsaparilla was a common medicine among cowboys for skin problems. Flips, a style of drink that employed a whole egg, were popular as a way to intake both alcohol and calories.

INGREDIENTS

1 ½ ounces reposado tequila

1 ounce tawny port

½ ounce sarsaparilla syrup

¼ ounce simple syrup

1 egg

1 dash orange bitters

DIRECTIONS

Shake the tequila, port, sarsaparilla syrup, simple syrup, egg, and bitters vigorously with ice. Strain into a mug or rocks glass.

 # RATTLESNAKE

The Rattlesnake is a known classic cocktail and appears in *The Savoy Cocktail Book* in 1930. Much too late to be a cowboy cocktail, you say? *The Savoy* also records Deadwood Dick's favorite drink (see page 107). We don't know exactly how old the Rattlesnake is, but it reads like a Western drink—a whiskey sour with a few bells and whistles. The two dashes of Peychaud's bitters represent the rattlesnake fangs.

INGREDIENTS

1 ½ ounces bourbon whiskey

½ ounce fresh lemon juice

½ ounce simple syrup

1 barspoon absinthe

1 egg white

2 dashes Peychaud's bitters,
   for garnish

DIRECTIONS

Shake the whiskey, lemon juice, simple syrup, absinthe, and egg white with ice. Strain into a cocktail glass and garnish with bitters.

High Plains Hellraiser

The High Plains are still one of the lowest-population-density regions in the US. A dry area that extends through western Nebraska and eastern Colorado, from Montana to Texas, it's an extended area of scrub brush, shortgrass prairie, and cacti. A few famed cities situated on the plains during the cowboy heyday were Cheyenne, Ogallala, and Dodge City. These were also among the roughest towns in the country, where lawmen were sparse. Liqueurs such as Luxardo maraschino and Benedictine traveled west as early as the Gold Rush and were used to flavor mixed drinks of all kinds. Mezcal was a popular spirit in the Southwest.

INGREDIENTS

2 ounces mezcal

1 ounce Luxardo maraschino liqueur

1 ounce fresh lime juice

¼ ounce Benedictine

1 dash Peychaud's bitters

DIRECTIONS

Shake the mezcal, maraschino liqueur, fresh lime juice, and Benedictine with ice. Strain into a cocktail glass and garnish with bitters.

I'm Your Huckleberry

Val Kilmer's deadpan delivery of the phrase "I'm your Huckleberry" as Doc Holliday in the 1993 film *Tombstone* made the saying famous. Surprisingly, Holliday actually said the words, and it meant something akin to "right man for the job." That is, if Johnny Ringo was looking for trouble, Holliday was more than happy to oblige.

Huckleberries were a treat found on the trail and they just so happen to pair well with whiskey. Huckleberry syrup is available in stores and online, including a fine version by Torani, the Italian maker of coffee syrups.

INGREDIENTS

2 ounces bourbon whiskey

1 ½ ounces huckleberry syrup

½ ounce fresh lemon juice

2 dashes Angostura bitters

Lemon twist, for garnish

DIRECTIONS

Shake the whiskey, huckleberry syrup, lemon juice, and bitters with ice. Strain into a cocktail glass and garnish with a lemon twist.

BROTHERS JAMES

Jesse and Frank James were notorious outlaws and, for nearly a decade after the Civil War, the most famous bandits in the West. Their bloodthirsty exploits left a trail of dead lawmen and civilians from Texas to Minnesota. While sometimes romanticized as American Robin Hoods, the brothers were simply criminals stealing for themselves.

Worcestershire sauce came to US shores in 1839 and was used to flavor meat as well as assist digestion. The bottles still sport the paper wrappers originally used to protect them on sea voyages. The sauce is now a classic pairing with tomato juice in Bloody Mary-style drinks.

INGREDIENTS

Hickory salt, for the glass rim

1 ounce bourbon whiskey

1 ounce reposado tequila

½ ounce fresh lime juice

3 ounces tomato juice

1 dash Worcestershire sauce

2 cocktail onions, for garnish

DIRECTIONS

Salt the rim of a rocks glass. Shake the whiskey, tequila, lime juice, tomato juice, and Worcestershire sauce with ice. Strain into the prepared glass filled with ice. Garnish with cocktail onions.

BILLY CAN

A billy can was a lightweight metal pot for making coffee. Just as it had fueled soldiers during the Civil War, hot coffee boosted morale on the cattle drives and was considered crucial to the success of an enterprise. This spicy version of an espresso martini will give you the fortitude to continue on up the trail in conditions both fair and foul.

INGREDIENTS

1 ounce reposado tequila

1 ounce Kahlúa

½ ounce Ancho Reyes

1 ounce espresso

DIRECTIONS

Shake the tequila, Kahlúa, Ancho Reyes, and espresso with ice. Strain into a cocktail glass.

PART 3

RED EYE

STIRRED DRINKS

"COURAGE IS BEING SCARED TO DEATH AND SADDLING UP ANYWAY."

JOHN WAYNE

Cocktails that contain spirits and liqueurs but not citrus, eggs, or dairy are generally stirred. This includes (contrary to some public opinion) martinis and Manhattans, as well as negronis. Because they are not diluted by citrus or dairy, the spirit-forward drinks in this section are great for getting the roundup started and encouraging serious contemplation as the ice melts. Beware the bite of the Mean Hombre (page 103) as well as the Bone Orchard (page 111). And if you can handle the gunfire of Thirty Shots in Thirty Seconds (page 120), you're a cowboy of considerable swagger.

Jack of Diamonds

"Jack of Diamonds" was a popular Texas cowboy song and it proclaimed the attributes of rye whiskey: "Whiskey, you villain/You've been my downfall/You've kicked me/You've cuffed me/But I love you for all." In card game lore, the Jack of Diamonds typically means good luck—although in varying versions he also represents the devil and deception. You'll just have to find out which is accurate with this fetching mix of whiskey and maraschino liqueur.

INGREDIENTS

2 ½ ounces rye whiskey

½ ounce Luxardo maraschino liqueur

Maraschino cherry, for garnish

DIRECTIONS

Stir the whiskey and maraschino liqueur with ice. Strain into a cocktail glass and garnish with a maraschino cherry.

Tombstone Tonsil Painter

By 1881, Tombstone, Arizona, was a boomtown boasting two dance halls and twenty saloons. In October of that year, marshal Virgil Earp, joined by his younger brothers, Wyatt and Morgan, and Doc Holliday, prevailed over the Clanton Gang at the O.K. Corral. Tonsil paint, or tonsil varnish, was a cowboy nickname for whiskey. Being a prosperous town, Tombstone bars would have featured more than a few liquor bottles for making fancy cocktails. Holliday, a dandy, would have liked this particular concoction.

INGREDIENTS

1 ½ ounces rye whiskey

1 ounce tawny port

¼ ounce Benedictine

2 dashes Angostura bitters

Maraschino cherry, for garnish

DIRECTIONS

Stir the whiskey, port, Benedictine, and bitters with ice. Strain into a cocktail glass and garnish with a maraschino cherry.

Mule Skinner

This is a historical cocktail of the Old West, a very popular blend of rye whiskey and crème de mûre, or blackberry liqueur. A mule skinner was a mule driver, and "skinner" meant someone who could outsmart the beasts and get them to do their bidding. Here, the original drink mix is improved upon with a dash of bitters. Cowboys liked their drinks and their food sugary whenever possible, so if the recipe is too sweet for your taste, try it with less crème de mûre.

INGREDIENTS

2 ounces rye whiskey

1 ounce crème de mûre

2 dashes mole or chocolate bitters (such as Bittermens)

Orange twist, for garnish

DIRECTIONS

Stir the whiskey, crème de mûre, and bitters with ice. Strain into a rocks glass with a large ice cube and garnish with an orange twist.

 Mean Hombre

There were plenty of mean hombres in the Wild West who were quick to, as the saying went, "get snorty." A special subset of the nasty gunslinger was the "kid," young men typically between seventeen and twenty-five who made their way in life through various delinquencies. These were not cowboys (unless there wasn't anything else to do for money), but rather characters that cowboys had to contend with in the various frontier towns. Buck-toothed and vicious Billy the Kid was the most famous of the bunch; there was also a Nevada Kid, Texas Kid, Jimmy the Kid, Pecos Kid, and so on. These "kids" were dangerous and sometimes fatal annoyances, and almost all invariably died young and un-mourned.

INGREDIENTS

1 ounce anejo tequila

1 ounce reposado tequila

¼ ounce Benedictine

1 dash orange bitters

Orange twist, for garnish

DIRECTIONS

Stir the tequilas, Benedictine, and bitters with ice. Strain into a rocks glass and garnish with an orange twist.

Fiddler's Bitch

To be as "drunk as a fiddler's bitch" was a rip-roaring time indeed. Violins were the most common instrument in the West; they were light, small, and easy to carry in the chuck wagon. A cowboy who could sing was a delight to his companions, and one who could play the violin was in very high demand on the trail and at festivals. Dance a little jig to this spirituous cocktail that will have you tuned up in no time at all.

INGREDIENTS

2 ounces brandy

1 ounce dry curaçao

¼ ounce Luxardo maraschino liqueur

DIRECTIONS

Stir the brandy, curaçao, and maraschino liqueur with ice. Strain into a cocktail glass.

CUSTER'S
LAST STAND

Frontier saloons typically featured oil paintings of patriotic subjects, sporting events, and sentimental scenes. The main attraction was often a giant image of a female nude over the bar. The most famous of these was in Denver—a reclining beauty that, by the trick of a couple attached hoses, the bartender could cause to heave her bosom. However, likely the most popular image of the era was *Custer's Last Fight* by artist Cassilly Adams, widely distributed by the Budweiser Beer Company in the 1880s. The hotly contested subject meant more beer sales for the saloon owners because Custer's folly was fodder for endless conversation and arguments (over more drinks).

DEADWOOD DICK

Said to be the favorite of Deadwood Dick himself, this is likely a period cocktail. Deadwood Dick, born Richard William Clark, was a hero of the Old West who worked for the famed Pony Express and fought with Custer at Little Bighorn. The man and the legend were famous enough that his drink appears in *The Savoy Cocktail Book* in 1930, recorded as a Yellow Daisy. It's not just a delightful drink, it also demonstrates cowboys' affinity for the finer things in life when they were available.

INGREDIENTS

1 ½ ounces Old Tom gin

1 ½ ounces dry vermouth

½ ounce Grand Marnier

1 dash absinthe

DIRECTIONS

Stir the gin, vermouth, Grand Marnier, and absinthe with ice. Strain into a cocktail glass.

WEST OF THE PECOS

Famed frontier judge Roy Bean advertised himself as the "only law West of the Pecos" and handed out justice from his saloon on the banks of the Rio Grande. He was famous for his lax and creative interpretation of the statutes. Once, when during a trial a lawyer said "*habeas corpus*," Bean, unfamiliar with the term, threatened to hang him for profanity. If Bean found you guilty, he would fine you whatever you had in your pockets and take the money. Drink to the colorful old judge with this easy sipper that won't have you cursing.

INGREDIENTS

2 ounces bourbon whiskey

1 ounce dry curaçao

1 ounce apple cider

DIRECTIONS

Stir the whiskey, curaçao, and apple cider with ice. Strain into a cocktail glass.

BOTTLED-IN-BOND

To be labeled bottled-in-bond, a liquor must be the product of one distiller in one distillation season, bottled at 100 proof (50% alcohol), and rest for four years in a federally bonded warehouse. The Bottled-in-Bond Act passed in 1897 to establish a quality standard for bourbon whiskey and rid liquor of additives such as burnt sugar, prune juice, tobacco, glycerin, and more.

BONE ORCHARD

Cowboys were known for their gallows humor, an example of which was their penchant for calling cemeteries "bone orchards." Cemeteries were also frequently dubbed "boot hill" (where all the boots are buried), such as the famed graveyard in Dodge City.

Applejack is one of the oldest spirits in the US, originally made by leaving hard cider outside to freeze and then scraping off the excess water—thus yielding a spirit. It was a process known as "jacking." Try this apple-y version of the familiar negroni alongside barbecue or a steak.

INGREDIENTS

1 ½ ounces bonded applejack
1 ½ ounces sweet vermouth
¾ ounce Campari

Orange twist, for garnish
Apple slice, for garnish

DIRECTIONS

Stir the applejack, sweet vermouth, and Campari with ice. Strain into a rocks glass with a large ice cube and garnish with an orange twist and an apple slice.

OLD CHISHOLM TRAIL

The Old Chisholm Trail was the most famous cattle trail after the Civil War, and was named after Jesse Chisholm, a Cherokee guide and rancher who scouted and developed the road. After being driven north on the trail, cattle were then shipped from Abilene, Kansas, to markets in the East. Chisholm died in 1864, before the cattle boom began, but was a key figure in the industry's history. He was inducted into the Hall of Great Westerners in 1974 and his grave in Oklahoma is listed on the National Register of Historic Places. The pecan is native to Texas and we can imagine Old Chisholm might have enjoyed this take on the Old Fashioned.

INGREDIENTS

2 ounces bourbon whiskey
¼ ounce Pecan Syrup (see recipe to the right)
1 dash Angostura bitters

DIRECTIONS

Stir the whiskey, Pecan Syrup, and bitters with ice. Strain into a rocks glass with a large ice cube.

FOR THE PECAN SYRUP

INGREDIENTS

1 cup (110 g) pecan halves
1 cup (237 g) water
1 cup (200 g) sugar

DIRECTIONS

In a saucepan, toast the pecans on medium-high heat until browning, 2 to 3 minutes. Add the water and sugar, stir, and bring to a boil. Reduce the heat and simmer the pecans for 5 minutes. Remove from the heat, let cool, and strain the syrup into a sealable container. This pecan syrup will keep for up to two weeks, sealed, in the refrigerator.

A WAY EAST: GUSTAVUS SWIFT

Meat—specifically beef, pork, and lamb—was the biggest US industry in the last half of the nineteenth century. Innovator (and former butcher) Gustavus Swift was an early proponent of refrigerated railcars, which eventually transformed the cattle industry by making it possible to ship dressed beef instead of live cattle. His streamlined processes in meatpacking facilities inspired Henry Ford's auto plants.

Dead or Alive

A wanted poster in the nineteenth century announced that a criminal was sought in connection with a crime and that a reward was on offer. The condition of the apprehended criminal was . . . optional. Theoretically, the law preferred a man to stand trial, but it was understood that resisting arrest often led to injuries. After the Civil War, most whiskey on the market was high-proof grain alcohol mixed with ingredients such as molasses and burnt sugar to make it palatable. A popular version employed prune juice. Plums and whiskey go well together, and this outré-looking (but fantastic-tasting) mix is good enough for the living and the dead.

INGREDIENTS

5 cocktail olives

2 ounces bourbon whiskey

½ ounce prune juice

¼ ounce simple syrup

1 dash Angostura bitters

DIRECTIONS

In a cocktail glass, muddle two of the olives. Add the whiskey, prune juice, simple syrup, and bitters with ice. Stir and strain into a rocks glass and garnish with the remaining cocktail olives.

 Robbers Roost

Because it was difficult to traverse and easy to defend, a small canyon in southeastern Utah became known as the "Robbers Roost." It was a favorite haunt of Butch Cassidy and his Wild Bunch, and the group was rumored to pass their time there by playing poker with twenty-dollar gold coins. Try this gold-inflected cocktail as you dream of all the secret caches Cassidy purportedly left in the surrounding hills.

INGREDIENTS

2 ounces bourbon whiskey

¾ ounce Goldschläger

1 dash orange bitters

Orange twist, for garnish

DIRECTIONS

Stir the whiskey, Goldschläger, and bitters with ice. Strain into a cocktail glass and garnish with an orange twist.

WRANGLER

A wrangler was responsible for all the horses used to work cattle. The term derives from the German word for "wrestle," likely because it was also the wrangler's job to tame the beasts. Luxardo maraschino cherries make a frequent appearance as a garnish in modern cocktails (think Manhattans), but their syrup is also a useful ingredient. For this drink, combine high-proof whiskey with cherry syrup and bitters for a true cowboy treat, ideal for relaxing after a long day breaking mustangs.

INGREDIENTS

2 ounces bonded bourbon whiskey

1 barspoon Luxardo maraschino cherry syrup

1 dash Tobacco bitters (such as 18.21 Bitters)

DIRECTIONS

Burn a small strip of oak, pecan, or hickory wood on a cutting board or other hard surface and place a rocks glass over it to collect the smoke. In a cocktail glass, stir the whiskey, cherry syrup, and bitters with ice. Strain into the prepared rocks glass filled with smoke.

Thirty Shots in Thirty Seconds

The shootout at the O.K. Corral is the cowboy era's most famous gunfight. But is it even possible that there was a shot fired every second, as the legend says? The shootout boasted six active participants and we know roughly how many times they squeezed their triggers: Doc Holliday shot two shotgun shells and then switched to his pistol. Billy Clanton emptied his gun. The Earps fired a few times, plus Frank McLaury got off a few shots before hitting the ground. Thirty is about right, and the sheer volume calls for a cocktail blaster of equal strength. Note: when the ingredients are layered using the back of a barspoon, this drink is as epic to behold as it is lively to consume. Pour gently and the liquors will separate naturally.

INGREDIENTS

1 ounce dry curaçao

1 ounce Fernet Branca

1 ounce bourbon whiskey

DIRECTIONS

Using a barspoon, layer the curaçao, Fernet Branca, and whiskey in a cold Nick and Nora or cocktail glass.

PART 4

ROUNDUP

COWBOY PUNCHES

"NO HOUR OF LIFE IS WASTED THAT IS SPENT
IN THE SADDLE."

WINSTON CHURCHILL

It is thought that the word "punch" comes from the Hindu word *paunch*, which means "five things"—in this case, liquor, sugar, water, citrus, and tea. The British invented punch in East India in the late seventeenth century and the mixed drink served in a large communal bowl quickly spread around the globe and to the American colonies. After the Revolutionary War, communal punch fell out of favor and morphed into a single glass of the good stuff served *à la minute*: the cocktail. By the Civil War, punches were still consumed at weddings, birthdays, anniversaries, and upon completion of a business deal. Think of these as large-format cocktails that make entertaining a cinch, because you can mix up a batch in advance.

CACTUS WINE

Originally a blend of mezcal and peyote, so-called "cactus wine" was popular along the Mexican border. This recipe is a less-hallucinogenic version that employs hibiscus syrup to stand in for wine. Lending a pleasing flavor and color to the drink, hibiscus is also high in vitamin C, and helped to prevent scurvy amongst cowboys.

INGREDIENTS

1 cup (187 g) reposado tequila

½ cup (163 g) Hibiscus Syrup (see page 55)

½ cup (118 g) fresh lime juice

3 cups (710 g) club soda

Lime slices, for garnish

Mint sprigs, for garnish

DIRECTIONS

In a serving bowl or large pitcher with ice, combine the tequila, Hibiscus Syrup, and lime juice, and stir. Add the club soda and stir gently. Garnish the individual cups with lime slices and sprigs of mint.

Estampida

Every attempt was made to calm the cattle herd at night in order to prevent a stampede. Lightning was a sure trigger, but an errant tumbleweed, the striking of a match, or even a loud sneeze could touch off an uncontrolled riot. Stampedes were dangerous—to everything in its path, and to the cattle themselves—and cowboys pursued the animals on their horses, firing shots in order to turn, halt, and regain order.

INGREDIENTS

1 ¼ cups (233 g) blanco tequila

¼ cup (47 g) mezcal

¾ cup (140 g) dry vermouth

¼ cup (59 g) lime juice

¼ cup (82 g) simple syrup

1 ½ cups (355 g) club soda

Lime slices, for garnish

DIRECTIONS

In a serving bowl or large pitcher with ice, combine the tequila, mezcal, vermouth, lime juice, and simple syrup, and stir. Add the club soda and stir gently. Garnish the individual glasses with a slice of lime.

Dodge House Punch

Doc Holliday opened his dental practice in the Dodge House Hotel in 1878. At the time, Dodge City was a small frontier town at the western end of the railroad track. The area became the cowboy capital for the next decade, and has the distinction of being where the term "red-light district" was coined. This rousing mix is named after the Doc's famed hotel, a simple two-story, unpainted wooden building that nevertheless functioned as a premier social hub.

INGREDIENTS

1 ½ cups (280 g) bourbon whiskey

½ cup (163 g) Pecan Syrup
(see page 112)

1 cup (237 g) fresh lemon juice

1 bottle sparkling wine

Lemon slices, for garnish

DIRECTIONS

In a serving bowl or large pitcher with ice, combine the whiskey, Pecan Syrup, and lemon juice, and stir. Add the sparkling wine and stir gently. Garnish the individual glasses with a lemon slice.

Taos Tanglefoot

The town of Taos, New Mexico, sits in the Sangre de Cristo Mountains—so-named in 1719 by a Spanish explorer because of their red-hued morning glow (Sangre de Cristo means "blood of Christ"). Taos was known in the cowboy era as the origin of Taos Lightning, a whiskey produced by the enterprising Simeon Turley. The liquor was made until 1847, when Turley was killed in the Taos Pueblo Revolt. Taos Lightning lived on as a term for zesty liquor for decades after. This tasty sangria variation is equally good cold on a hot day or warmed for a cold night.

INGREDIENTS

1 bottle red wine

⅓ cup (108 g) agave nectar

2 ounces lime juice

4 cinnamon sticks, for garnish

DIRECTIONS

In a serving bowl or large pitcher with ice, combine the wine, agave nectar, and lime juice, and stir. Garnish with cinnamon sticks.

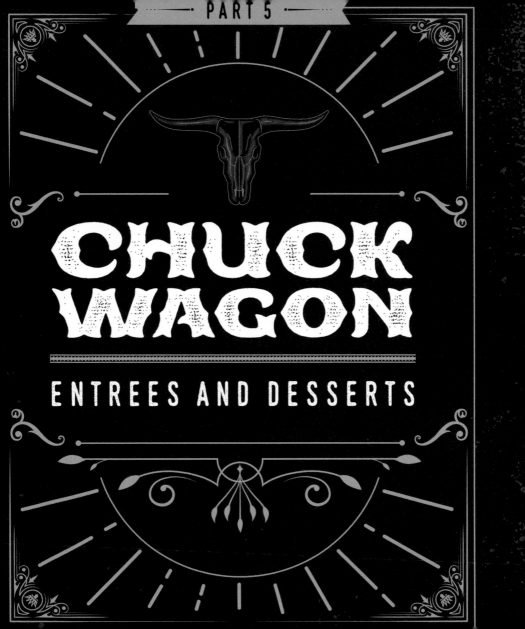

PART 5

CHUCK WAGON

ENTREES AND DESSERTS

Charles Goodnight of the famed Goodnight-Loving Trail (see page 32) invented the chuck wagon in 1866 by converting an army surplus Studebaker. The wagons—and the irascible field chefs who went with them—were a headache on the long journeys over rough terrain. Prone to getting stuck in mud and breaking up in rushing waters, the wagons were nevertheless essential for carrying all the cowboy gear and food. Range fare tended to be grim, but cattle outfits knew that an able chef kept the workers loyal and as happy as possible on the harsh job. Typical fare included pinto beans, beef, molasses, cornmeal, biscuits, gravy, and coffee. The addition of wild onions, harvested along the way and high in vitamin C, prevented scurvy.

Cowboy cooking is Dutch oven cooking. It also means cooking mostly without eggs, fresh fruit, fresh vegetables, or sugar. When cowboys made a rare foray into town, the first thing they did (after washing up) was seek out oysters and eggs—and sweets. Saloons at the time offered so-called "free lunch," small gratis items that came with a drink (see page 139). In this chapter, you will find a number of popular cowboy dishes suitable for any occasion, from ever-present ranch beans to a popular eggless cake.

# Corn Dodgers

· SERVES 4–6 ·

At their simplest, corn dodgers were balls of cornmeal and bacon grease cooked in a Dutch oven. They were easy to handle and provided calories for cowboys on the go. Stale dodgers were later made into mush, and if they were truly past their prime, were fed to the horses. Today, there is a bit of disagreement over whether dodgers were a dumpling, or if they were what we know today as hush puppies. Both styles are correct. This recipe hews toward the latter because fried cornmeal is a particularly excellent cocktail accompaniment.

INGREDIENTS

1 cup (125 g) all-purpose flour

1 cup (125 g) cornmeal

1 tablespoon baking powder

1 tablespoon baking soda

1 tablespoon sugar

1 tablespoon onion powder

1 teaspoon kosher salt

1 cup (242 g) buttermilk

2 eggs

Peanut or vegetable oil, for frying

DIRECTIONS

In a medium-size bowl, combine the flour, cornmeal, baking powder, baking soda, sugar, onion powder, and salt. In a large bowl, combine the buttermilk and eggs. Add dry ingredients to the wet ingredients and stir to incorporate. In a Dutch oven or saucepan, heat the oil.

Form the mixture into golf ball-size fritters, then drop into the hot oil and cook for 3 to 4 minutes, or until golden brown and crispy. Using a slotted spoon or tongs, transfer to a wire rack or large plate lined with paper towels and let drain before serving.

Ranch Beans

Beans were a cowboy staple, and dried beans comprised a large portion of the chuck box that accompanied any cattle outfit. This is a rich, flavorful, soul-satisfying recipe that makes it understandable how the lowly bean can be a stand-in for more substantial fare. These go well with any barbecue but can be a main course.

INGREDIENTS

- 4 ancho chiles, stems and seeds removed
- 3 15-ounce (245-gram) cans pinto beans, drained and rinsed
- 3 cups (720 g) beef broth, divided
- 1 tablespoon vegetable oil

- ½ large onion, diced
- 6 cloves garlic, minced
- 1 15-ounce (245-gram) can diced tomatoes and their juices
- 1 teaspoon light brown sugar

- 1 teaspoon apple cider vinegar
- 1 teaspoon paprika
- 1 teaspoon ground cumin
- 1 teaspoon dried oregano
- 1 tablespoon kosher salt

DIRECTIONS

In a large skillet or sauté pan over medium-high heat, cook the anchos on each side for 2 minutes, transfer to a bowl of warm water, and rehydrate for 20 minutes.

In a Dutch oven or stock pot, add the pinto beans and 2 cups of the beef broth. Bring the pot to a boil, reduce the heat, cover, and simmer, stirring occasionally, for 15 minutes. In a skillet or sauté pan over medium heat, heat the vegetable oil and cook the onions for 5 minutes. Add the garlic and cook for another minute. Transfer the onions and garlic to a blender and add the tomatoes, brown sugar, apple cider vinegar, paprika, cumin, oregano, salt, the remaining 1 cup of beef broth, and hydrated ancho chiles. Puree until smooth.

Stir the chile puree into the beans and continue to cook the beans, uncovered, for another hour, or until the beans are tender and the sauce has reduced.

CHILI STEAKS

· MAKES 2 ·

Slap this spice blend on any steak and raise the flavor to a high pitch. If you're a purist and believe that very little adds to a great steak other than salt, black pepper, and a little butter, this rub will change your mind. It is an easy recipe to make in advance; try doubling it so you have some already on hand next time.

INGREDIENTS

1 teaspoon ancho chile powder

½ teaspoon chili powder

½ teaspoon freshly ground
   black pepper

1 teaspoon sea salt

1 tablespoon unsalted butter

2 roughly one-pound (454-gram)
   New York strip steaks

DIRECTIONS

In a small bowl, combine the ancho chile powder, chili powder, black pepper, and salt. Rub the mixture into all sides of both steaks. Heat a cast-iron skillet or sauté pan on high heat. Add the butter, swirling the pan to coat. Place the steaks in the skillet and cook the first side for 3 to 4 minutes. Turn the steaks and cook for 3 to 4 minutes on the second side. Using tongs, briefly cook the edges of the steaks and remove to a wood surface or serving plates to rest for 10 minutes before serving.

★ FREE LUNCH

During the cowboy era, American saloons offered "free lunch," or small bites served gratis alongside drink orders. A typical free lunch included smoked oysters, crackers with Limburger cheese, rye bread, and sardines. If you want to recreate a free lunch and make it a feast, add salted peanuts, sauerkraut, cold cuts, pretzels, and dill pickles. Crafty saloon owners knew that such salty offerings not only kept customers around longer but kept them thirsty for more.

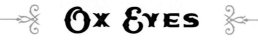

Ox Eyes

Also called "Eggs in Hell" or "Eggs in Purgatory," Ox Eyes are a classic Southwest breakfast dish that work as a snack any time. The combination betrays its Spanish influence, and likely originated from a version of huevos rancheros. The recipe's simple mix of tomato, green bell pepper, and onion yields something that is more than the sum of its parts—and makes for a great bite with mixed drinks.

INGREDIENTS

1 tablespoon unsalted butter

½ medium onion, diced

½ green bell pepper, seeded and diced

½ jalapeno chile, stemmed, seeded, and minced

1 15-ounce (245-gram) can pureed tomatoes

¼ teaspoon kosher salt

4 eggs

DIRECTIONS

Heat the butter in a skillet or saucepan over medium heat. Add the onion, bell pepper, and jalapeno, and sauté until the onions are softened and translucent. Add the tomatoes and salt, and bring to a boil. Break the eggs into the mixture, cover, and cook until the whites are set but the yolks are still soft, about 4 minutes. Serve with toast or potatoes and strong coffee.

COWBOY STEW

· MAKES 6 SERVINGS ·

The original range stew recipes contained less-than-desirable animal parts such as stomach, tongue, and brain. This was known as "Son of a Bitch" stew, and cowboys adored it. This recipe below does away with the nasty bits and instead employs beef chuck. Cattle in the late nineteenth century were lean, so the meat was best enjoyed after a long braise, such as in a stew. This particular version assumes you have a mighty fine chuck wagon cook who carries thyme, mustard, and bay leaf in the spice box.

INGREDIENTS

2 tablespoons vegetable oil

2 pounds (908 g) beef chuck, cut into ¼-inch cubes

1 onion, diced

4 garlic cloves

1 bay leaf

1 teaspoon dried thyme

1 teaspoon dried mustard

1 teaspoon ground black pepper

1 teaspoon kosher salt

6 waxy potatoes, diced

6 carrots, peeled and diced

½ cabbage, shredded

4 cups (960 g) beef stock

DIRECTIONS

In a large Dutch oven over medium–high heat, heat the vegetable oil, then add the beef cubes and cook until browned on all sides, about 5 minutes. Using a slotted spoon, transfer the browned beef to a bowl.

Lower heat to medium and add the onion, cooking until translucent and slightly browned. Add the garlic, bay leaf, thyme, dried mustard, black pepper, and salt and cook, stirring constantly, for 1 minute.

Return the beef to the pot and add the potatoes, carrots, cabbage, and beef stock. Bring to a boil and reduce to a simmer. Simmer, partially covered, for 2 hours or until beef is tender, adding water if necessary.

CHILI POWDER

German immigrant William Gebhardt first pulverized dried chile peppers by using a meat grinder in the 1890s. The powder was popularized along the Wells Fargo stagecoach line in Texas and became a boon to home cooks and chuck wagon chefs alike. The powder also helped popularize chili as a recognizable dish across the US.

CHILI CON CARNE

Chili Con Carne in its modern form likely originated in the early nineteenth century. San Antonio's so-called "chili queens" made huge quantities in their homes and sold individual portions at makeshift outdoor tables. However, the recipe may be far older; "chili" originates from an Aztec word, and Spanish friars recorded eating stews with peppers and spices as early as the 1500s. Chili Con Carne is the official dish of Texas, and the longstanding cowboy favorite is now known around the world.

INGREDIENTS

1 tablespoon cumin seeds

2 tablespoons vegetable oil

2 pounds (908 g) boneless
beef chuck, cut into
¼-inch cubes

1 large white onion, chopped

3 tablespoons chili powder

2 teaspoons paprika

1 teaspoon black pepper

½ teaspoon kosher salt

5 garlic cloves, minced

2 cups (480 g) beef stock

1 28-ounce (794-gram) can
pureed tomatoes

2 ancho chiles, stems
removed and seeded

DIRECTIONS

In a large Dutch oven over medium heat, toast the cumin seeds. Remove the seeds to a mortar and pestle or onto a work surface and crush.

Return the Dutch oven to medium-high heat and heat the vegetable oil. Add the beef cubes and cook until browned on all sides, about 5 minutes. Using a slotted spoon, transfer the beef to a bowl. Lower heat to medium and add the onions, cooking until translucent and slightly browned. Add the chili powder, paprika, black pepper, salt, and garlic and cook, stirring constantly, for 1 minute. Add the stock, tomatoes, and chiles, and return the beef to the pot. Bring to a boil and reduce to simmer. Simmer, partially covered, for 2 hours, or until the beef is tender, adding water if necessary.

After simmering, remove the anchos and puree them using a blender or food processor. Return the pureed anchos to the pot, stir to combine, and serve.

Cow Camp Beef Macaroni

· MAKES 6 SERVINGS ·

Both pre-packaged chili powder and dried macaroni were available by the late nineteenth century and were employed on the cattle trail. There is very little as satisfying after a hard day's work as this straightforward pasta, meat, and spice recipe. It's meant to feed an army of hungry cowboys, and is both great campfire and party food.

INGREDIENTS

- 6 cups (1420 g) salted water
- 1 pound (150 g) elbow macaroni
- 2 teaspoons cumin seeds
- 1 tablespoon vegetable oil
- 1 pound (454 g) ground beef

- 1 medium white onion, finely chopped
- 1 jalapeno pepper, seeded and minced
- 1 tablespoon Worcestershire sauce

- 2 tablespoons chili powder
- 1 teaspoon dried oregano
- 1 teaspoon ground black pepper
- 1 ½ teaspoons kosher salt

DIRECTIONS

In a large stockpot, bring the salted water to a boil. Cook the elbow macaroni in the boiling water according to the package instructions and drain.

Meanwhile, in a cast-iron skillet or sauté pan over medium heat, toast the cumin seeds. Remove the seeds to a mortar and pestle or onto a work surface and crush.

In a skillet or sauté pan over medium-high heat, heat the vegetable oil and add the beef, cooking until browned, 7 to 10 minutes. Transfer to a bowl using a slotted spoon. In the same skillet, add the onion and jalapeno, and cook until the onion is translucent. Return the beef to the skillet and add the ground cumin seeds, Worcestershire sauce, chili powder, oregano, black pepper, and salt, and reduce heat to low. Combine the macaroni with the beef mixture and serve.

Jerky Gravy

· MAKES 4–6 SERVINGS ·

The word "jerky" comes from the Spanish word *charqui*, which denoted long strips of meat air-dried in the sun. Preserved protein was a boon to travelers and, broken down in a roux, makes for a fantastic cowboy gravy over bread or other starches. This is ideal campfire grub, but tasty enough to serve at Sunday brunch.

INGREDIENTS

1 cup (90 g) beef jerky

2 tablespoons butter

1 tablespoon flour

2 cups (490 g) whole milk

DIRECTIONS

Using a mortar and pestle or a meat tenderizer on a work surface, pound the jerky to shreds. In a medium saucepan over medium-high heat, melt the butter and add the jerky. Cook until the butter is browning and then add the flour. Stir into a roux with the butter and slowly add the milk. The gravy should coat the stirring spoon. Serve over biscuits or fried potatoes.

 SPOTTED PUP

This simple rice pudding recipe was a special treat for cowboys. Traditionally, it would have been made without fresh milk; canned condensed milk appeared as a military ration as early as the 1860s and was the go-to. However, this recipe uses both fresh milk and an egg because the addition makes for a rich pudding that can handle the extra whiskey. This recipe is both decadent and comforting.

INGREDIENTS

⅓ cup (59 g) white rice

2 ½ cups (612 g) whole milk

1 tablespoon salted butter

1 egg

¼ cup (49 g) brown sugar

1 teaspoon vanilla extract

1 tablespoon whiskey

½ cup (73 g) raisins

¼ teaspoon ground nutmeg

¼ teaspoon ground cinnamon

DIRECTIONS

In a medium saucepan, bring the rice, milk, and butter to a boil over medium-high heat. Reduce the heat to low and simmer until the rice is tender, about 20 to 25 minutes, stirring frequently. In a small mixing bowl, whisk together the egg and brown sugar. Add a tablespoon of the hot rice mixture to the egg mixture, whisking vigorously. Repeat two more times until the egg mixture is tempered. Add the egg mixture back into the rice and milk mixture and stir, on low heat, for 5 to 10 minutes, until thickened. Do not boil or it will curdle. Stir in the vanilla and whiskey. Remove from heat and stir in the raisins, nutmeg, and cinnamon.

 # EGGLESS CAKE

Frontier cooks improvised many desserts that did not require eggs, and this is one of the more famous recipes. It is a spice cake that harkens back to New Orleans or Caribbean origins, and is especially good with cocktails or strong coffee. It's so rich and decadent, you won't miss the eggs.

INGREDIENTS

4 tablespoons butter,
plus extra for greasing

2 cups (473 g) water

2 cups (389 g) brown sugar

1 teaspoon kosher salt

½ teaspoon ground cinnamon

½ teaspoon ground allspice

1 tablespoon cocoa powder

1 cup (145 g) raisins

3 cups (376 g) all-purpose flour

2 teaspoons baking soda

DIRECTIONS

Preheat the oven to 350°F (180°C; gas mark 4) and grease a 9 by 5-inch loaf pan. In a Dutch oven or medium saucepan, bring the water, butter, sugar, salt, cinnamon, allspice, cocoa powder, and raisins to a boil. Simmer for 5 minutes and let cool. In a large bowl, combine the flour and baking soda. Stir the wet ingredients into the dry and transfer the mixture to the prepared loaf pan. Bake for 1 hour.

Molasses Cake

Molasses was a popular and available sweetener, and this cake would have been known and sought out during stops in cattle towns. Rich and moist, the recipe is ace with cocktails of all kinds. It is also a cinch to make for a crowd. Top with toasted nuts and whipped cream for added delight.

INGREDIENTS

2 tablespoons butter, plus extra for greasing

½ cup (100 g) sugar

2 eggs

1 cup (327 g) molasses

½ cup (118 g) water

½ teaspoon baking soda

2 cups (250 g) flour

DIRECTIONS

Preheat the oven to 350˚F (180˚C; gas mark 4) and grease a 9 by 9-inch baking pan. In a large bowl, cream the butter and sugar. Add the eggs and stir to combine. In a medium bowl, mix the molasses, water, and baking soda. Add alternately with the flour to the creamed butter mixture. Transfer to the prepared pan and bake for 45 minutes.

Dried Apple Pie

Dried apples were a cowboy staple and readily available. The trick is to reconstitute the dried slices in water and then use them much like fresh ones. Because the apple flavor is intensified by drying, it may rival your favorite just-picked version. Cowboys consumed apple pie in abundance and with relish, sometimes accompanied with a slice of cheese.

INGREDIENTS

2 cups (338 g) dried apples

2 ½ cups (592 g) water

¼ cup (50 g) granulated sugar

1 tablespoon all-purpose flour

1 teaspoon ground cinnamon

¼ teaspoon ground nutmeg

¼ teaspoon kosher salt

1 9-inch pie pastry shell

DIRECTIONS

Preheat the oven to 375°F (190°C; gas mark 5). Boil the dried apples in the water for 15 minutes until softened and drain. Add the sugar, flour, cinnamon, nutmeg, and salt, and transfer the mixture to the pie crust. Cover loosely with foil and bake for 1 hour.

TRAIL KIT
PANTRY RECOMMENDATIONS, TOOLS, AND TECHNIQUES

STOCK YOUR PANTRY

Like a cook keeping the chuck wagon stocked, you're going to want to make sure you have the essentials on hand.

BITTERS

Today there are a huge variety of bitters available. Angostura, Peychaud's, and orange bitters are all employed in classic cocktails and in this book—and are worth keeping on hand. In addition, this book recommends tobacco bitters such as 18.21.

OLIVES

Spanish Manzanilla olives were the standard in cocktails such as martinis for a long time. These days, Castelvetrano olives are appearing frequently at US bars.

COCKTAIL ONIONS

Cocktail onions appear in the Gibson but also in Bloody Marys and other drinks that have a savory note. In this book, they are employed in the Brothers James (page 91).

COCKTAIL CHERRIES

Over the past number of years, Amarena cherries have supplanted fake-red-dye cocktail cherries. There are, however, a few brands that do make decent maraschino cherries—like Luxardo and Tillen Farms—and they are worth seeking out.

CLUB SODA

Carbonated water, seltzer, and club soda aren't quite as similar as one might think. Club soda includes additives such as sodium and potassium that lend additional flavor to drinks; it is the preferred choice in cocktails.

EGGS

To prevent the shells from getting into your drink, crack the egg on a counter surface and not on the edge of a glass.

Note: If you have a compromised immune system, use pasteurized eggs or powdered egg whites as an alternative to fresh eggs; two teaspoons powder to one ounce water will yield the equivalent to a single egg white.

ICE

Ice is often overlooked as an ingredient in cocktails, but it is one of the most important details. Beware that ice can take on flavors from your freezer, so be sure to make it fresh. Using filtered water can also improve taste. For added presentation, consider investing in a few silicon trays. They are an inexpensive way to improve your cocktail game.

AGAVE NECTAR

Agave nectar and agave syrup are not necessarily interchangeable. While agave syrup is made from the sugar in the agave plant's leaves, agave nectar is made by reducing the agave plant's sap. Agave syrup tends to be richer and more intense, making it ideal for applications such as baking. Agave nectar is preferred for drinks. However, in a pinch, substituting them works.

TOOLS OF THE TRADE

Crafting cocktails does not require a lot of fancy or expensive equipment, but there are a few items that will make your drinks mixing easier and improve their quality.

JIGGER

Measuring precisely is a must when creating craft drinks. There are a number of options available on the market; the OXO jigger is ideal for most home bartenders.

BOSTON SHAKER

The classic three-part shaker, often called a martini shaker, is not ideal for making most cocktails. It is frequently too small and the lid sticks when the metal gets cold. The two-part Boston shaker is preferred. Originally composed of a metal tin and a pint glass, today the two parts are often both metal for safety. Two-part metal shakers are now widely available in kitchen stores and online.

MIXING GLASSES

Mixing glasses are used for all stirred drinks. They are necessary for making stirred drinks correctly, but any vessel will work in a pinch. Glasses have come down in price dramatically in the past few years and are widely available in specialty stores and online.

BARSPOON

A barspoon is required to make properly stirred cocktails. Find one with enough heft at the end of the handle to crack ice; they are widely available in kitchen stores and online.

STRAINERS

There are two styles of cocktail strainers: Hawthorne and julep. Hawthorne strainers (a flat disc with a coiled spring) are employed for shaken drinks, while julep strainers (slightly incurved disc with no spring) are used for stirred cocktails. If you are in doubt, buy a Hawthorne, which works well for both purposes.

CITRUS PRESS

Hand juicers are ideal for making small amounts of juice, but it is nice to have a larger juicer with a reservoir. It may be worth investing in a quality electric juicer if you are making a lot of drinks for cocktail parties.

Y-PEELER

A y-peeler, sometimes called a Swiss peeler, is the preferred tool for citrus skin.

MUDDLER

A muddler should be made of unstained, nonreactive wood. Avoid paint, plastic, or metal.

GLASSWARE

No special glassware is required to enjoy a good drink. However, the average size for a proper cocktail is small when poured into commonly available glassware. When acquiring cocktail-specific glasses, your first choice should likely be a set of coupe glasses—sometimes called champagne glasses—which are now widely available online. The best size for these is between four and six ounces. Additionally, highball and rocks glasses can improve presentation.

OTHER ITEMS THAT ARE USEFUL WHEN PREPARING COCKTAILS

- ⋆ Cutting board
- ⋆ Paring knife
- ⋆ Bottle opener
- ⋆ Wine key
- ⋆ Squeeze bottles (for citrus juice)
- ⋆ Microplane grater
- ⋆ Funnel
- ⋆ Large-format ice cube trays
- ⋆ Ice bucket and scoop
- ⋆ Hand towels
- ⋆ Cocktail picks

TECHNIQUES

Once you've mastered these basics, you'll be well on your way to becoming the fastest bartender in the West.

MEASURE

Use a jigger to measure ingredients. This ensures a consistent, balanced drink every time—and you can recalibrate with precision if something is too sweet or too sour. Free-pour later if you really think you've nailed your recipes and technique.

ICE AND ICE TRAYS

Ice is crucial to cocktail making. Be sure to use fresh ice, as ice can take on "off" flavors from your freezer if stored too long. It helps to use filtered water. Silicone ice trays will allow you to make perfect squares and large cubes (see tool recommendations, page 161).

GARNISH

A garnish is not just for looks. A spritz of lemon zest over a drink adds aroma and flavor—and changes the cocktail. Have your garnish handy so you're not looking for it after you've already made a drink.

FRESH CITRUS

Fresh citrus will enliven your cocktails immeasurably. Do not use bottled juice. See tool recommendations for citrus presses, page 161.

HOW TO RINSE A GLASS

Rinsing a glass with a liqueur imparts flavor without overpowering the drink. Add a barspoon of spirit to a glass, then tilt the glass and roll it to evenly distribute the spirit and coat the inside. Discard the extra liquid—or don't, depending on your preference.

CREATING A SALT OR SUGAR RIM

Run the edge of a citrus wedge along the lip of a glass so the juice moistens the rim. Invert the glass and dip it onto a plate of salt or sugar. Tap the glass to remove the excess.

WHEN TO STIR

Cocktails that are made up of spirits—think martinis and Manhattans—are stirred. Combine stirred cocktails and ice in a mixing glass and stir with a barspoon until the cocktail is chilled, at least thirty-five to forty seconds.

WHEN TO SHAKE

When a cocktail recipe calls for citrus, eggs, or milk, combine the ingredients in a shaker with ice and shake vigorously. To prevent ice shivs or other particles in the cocktail, strain the drink using a Hawthorne strainer (see page 160).

HOW TO MUDDLE

Drinks with citrus, sugar cubes, or herbs such as mint are sometimes muddled. When muddling herbs, use a wooden muddler (see page 161).

HOW TO BATCH COCKTAILS FOR A PARTY

Convert the ounces in any cocktail recipe to cups for a larger version.

COMMON COCKTAIL RATIOS FOR CREATING YOUR OWN DRINKS

Classic cocktail recipes are time-tested ratios that work. However, after making a few hundred classics, you may be ready to strike out on your own. Two established ratios for making your own cocktails from scratch are below:

The 2:1:1

2 ounces base spirit

1 ounce sour (citrus)

1 ounce sweet liqueur
  (or simple syrup)

Dash of aromatics, such as bitters

The 3:2:1

3 ounces base spirit

2 ounces sweet or sour

1 ounce sweet or sour

Dash of aromatics, such as bitters

FINE
GATHERINGS

HOME ON THE RANGE

There isn't much better in life than sleeping out under the stars, whether you've spent a long day in the saddle or just want to enjoy the great outdoors with your nearest and dearest. The cowboy staples on this food menu can easily be shared around the campfire, and the drinks summon up the wide vistas and natural beauty of the wild frontier.

FOOD MENU

Corn Dodgers 134

Ranch Beans 137

Cowboy Stew 142

Cow Camp Beef Macaroni 146

DRINK MENU

Frontier Scamper Juice 23

Cast-Iron Julep 36

Velvet Couch 63

Cimarron 67

Boss of the Plains 68

FOR THE GAMBLER

Transport your guests back to the saloons of old with this spread—and maybe make a buck or two, if Lady Luck is kind. Pair your preferred poison with a classic game of poker and imagine you're in one of the saloons of Deadwood or Tombstone.

FOOD MENU

Corn Dodgers 134

Chili Steaks 138

DRINK MENU

Dead Man's Hand 20

Green Cloth 59

Tiger's Tail 75

Dodge House Punch 128

A HORSE WITH NO NAME

Horses were the main mode of transportation in the Old West, helping their riders traverse hundreds of miles of open trails. (Though whether they were riding off to a legitimate job or fleeing the law is another story.) Pull on your boots and grab your Stirrup Cup—it's time to saddle up!

FOOD MENU

Corn Dodgers 134

Cowboy Stew 142

DRINK MENU

Stirrup Cup 16

Lucky Horseshoe 44

Swing Rider 48

Broncobuster 52

SWEETHEARTS OF THE WEST

Life on the frontier wasn't all about the men. If you're looking to celebrate the famous ladies who headed up saloons and rode the dusty trails from Montana to Texas, let these menus be your guide. Everything here is sweet, but just a little bit dangerous, and the Chili Con Carne pays homage to the chili queens of yesteryear.

FOOD MENU

Chili Con Carne 145

Eggless Cake 153

Molasses Cake 154

Dried Apple Pie 157

DRINK MENU

Watermelon Ranch Water 27

Madame Mustache 39

Thorny Rose 64

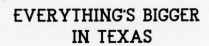

EVERYTHING'S BIGGER
IN TEXAS

From the wide-open skies to the generous helpings of delicious meals, everything truly is bigger in Texas. You can bring a bit of the Lone Star State into your own home with these menus. And, of course, what kind of Texas-themed gathering would it be without Chili Con Carne, the state dish?

FOOD MENU

Ox Eyes 141

Chili Con Carne 145

Cow Camp Beef Macaroni 146

Spotted Pup 150

DRINK MENU

Buffalo Gap 19

G.T.T. G&T 28

Goodnight Loving 32

Old Chisholm Trail 112

WANTED DEAD OR ALIVE

Criminals like Jesse and Frank James and Billy the Kid are still known the world over for their Old West exploits. Whether you want to host a costume party featuring a rogues' gallery of frontier criminals or impress your friends with tales of dastardly deeds, make sure to do it with a Necktie Social in hand.

FOOD MENU

Chili Steaks 138

Eggless Cake 153

Dried Apple Pie 157

DRINK MENU

Belly Through the Brush 24

Necktie Social 40

High Plains Hellraiser 87

Brothers James 91

Dead or Alive 115

ACKNOWLEDGMENTS

A big thank-you goes to my editor Katie McGuire for her suggestions on this mighty fine project. Plus, a tip of the hat is offered to my agent Clare Pelino for her wise counsel. A warm thanks goes to Kevin Lundell of Broad Street Beverage Co. for assistance testing drinks in this book; there is no better company for heading up the cocktail trail.

Finally, a debt of gratitude is owed to my partner Janine Hawley, who joined me on a research trip to Texas, listened to me talk endlessly about cowboys, and helped recipe test the grub herein.

ABOUT THE AUTHOR

André Darlington is a former restaurant critic and restaurateur turned award-winning beverage writer. He is the best-selling author of ten cocktail books, including *The Unofficial Big Lebowski Cocktail Book*, *Gotham City Cocktails*, *Booze Cruise*, and *Bar Menu*. He lives in Greensboro, North Carolina.

SELECT BIBLIOGRAPHY

Adams, Andy, *The Log of a Cowboy: A Narrative of the Old Trail Days*, Compass Circle, 2019

Arthur, Timothy, *Ten Nights in a Bar-Room and What I Saw There*, J.W. Bradley, 1854

Bonney, Edward, *Banditti of the Prairies: A Tale of the Mississippi Valley*, Wildside Press, 2021

Brands, H.W., *Dreams of El Dorado*, Basic Books, 2020

Craddock, Harry, *The Savoy Cocktail Book*, Pavilion Books, 2011

Davis, William C., *The Civil War Cookbook*, Courage Books, 1993

Drawbaugh, Dean, *A Soldier's Cookbook 1863*, Drawbaugh Publishing Group, 2013

Erdoes, Richard, *Saloons of the Old West*, Gramercy Books, 1979

Hughes, Stella, *Chuck Wagon Cookin'*, University of Arizona Press, 1974

Knowlton, Christopher, *Cattle Kingdom: The Hidden History of the Cowboy West*, Mariner Books, 2017

Love, Nat, *The Life and Adventures of Nat Love*, University of Nebraska Press, 1995

Mayo, Matthew P., *Cowboys, Mountain Men, and Grizzly Bears: Fifty of the Grittiest Moments in the History of the Wild West*, Twodot, 2009

Sides, Hampton, *Blood and Thunder: The Epic Story of Kit Carson and the Conquest of the American West*, Anchor Books, 2007

Spaulding, Lily May and John Spaulding, ed., *Civil War Recipes: Receipts from the Pages of Godey's Lady's Book*, University Press of Kentucky, 1999

Wagner, Tricia Martineau, *Black Cowboys of the Old West*, Twodot, 2011

Walsh, Robb, *The Tex-Mex Cookbook*, Broadway Books, 2004

Webb, Walter Prescott, *The Great Plains*, University of Nebraska Press, 1981

Wister, Owen, *The Virginian*, Compass Circle, 2019

INDEX